MOROCCO

COUNTRY EXPLORERS

Robin Nelson

Lerner Publications Company • Minneapolis

Lerner Publications Company
A division of Lerner Publishing Group, Inc.
241 First Avenue North
Minneapolis, MN 55401 U.S.A.

Website address: www.lernerbooks.com

Library of Congress Cataloging-in-Publication Data

Nelson, Robin, 1971–
    Morocco / by Robin Nelson.
        p.   cm. — (Country explorers)
    Includes index.
    ISBN 978–0–7613–6419–1 (lib. bdg. : alk. paper)
    1. Morocco—Juvenile literature. I. Title.
    DT305.N45 2012
    964—dc22   2010044475

Manufactured in the United States of America
1 – MG – 7/15/11

Table of Contents

Welcome!

You've come to Morocco! This country's official name is the Kingdom of Morocco. But most people just call it Morocco.

The country sits on the northwest corner of the continent of Africa. Western Sahara lies to the south. Along its eastern border, Morocco touches Algeria. The Atlantic Ocean lies to the west. To the north is the Mediterranean Sea.

The Atlantic Ocean crashes into the ancient walls of this western Moroccan city.

Looking at Europe

Morocco is only about 9 miles (14 kilometers) away from the continent of Europe. The Strait of Gibraltar separates Morocco from the European country of Spain.

This photo of Morocco was taken from Spain. The waterway in the photo is the Strait of Gibraltar.

Many Moroccans take a ferry across the strait to go to Spain. The Strait of Gibraltar flows between the Mediterranean Sea and the Atlantic Ocean.

Map Whiz Quiz

Take a look at the map on page 5. A map is a drawing or a chart of a place. Trace the outline of the map onto a sheet of paper. Look for Spain. Mark it with an *N* for north. Can you find Western Sahara? Mark it with an *S* for south. The Atlantic Ocean lies to the west. Mark it with a *W*. Find Algeria. Mark it with an *E* for east. Color Morocco yellow. Color the Atlantic Ocean and the Mediterranean Sea blue.

A ferry docks at the Moroccan city of Tangier on the Strait of Gibraltar.

Western Sahara

Western Sahara is a territory, not a country. Morocco claims Western Sahara. It's mostly desert. Only about five hundred thousand people live there.

These people are walking in the desert in Western Sahara.

But the people of Western Sahara want to be an independent country. Morocco wants the territory's natural resources. Over time, control of this land has caused many battles and arguments.

The Atlantic Coast of Western Sahara has great fishing.

The Coast and the Plains

Let's go to the beach! Moroccans enjoy miles of sandy beaches along the Atlantic Ocean. The Mediterranean coast offers a mix of sandy and rocky beaches with many cliffs.

Tangier

Dear Zach,

Hello from Morocco! We are having a great trip! Today we visited Tangier. It is a city on the coast. We went to an outdoor market and bought pastries and fresh tangerines. Later, we went to the beach. Tomorrow we're going to the port to watch ships come and go.

See you soon,

Avery

The land gets green and flat inland from the coast. Most Moroccans live here on the plains. The weather is a little cooler than along the coast. The plains also get more rain.

Inland Morocco has grassy plains.

Mules in the Mountains

Many people who live in Morocco's mountains raise mules. They help mountain people with their work. Mules are stronger than horses. Mules also work better in hot weather. They don't need much to eat. And they don't get sick very often.

Mountains and Desert

The Atlas Mountains cover much of Morocco in three sections. In the far south are the Anti-Atlas. Central Morocco has the Grand and Middle Atlas Mountains. In the winter, snow covers the mountains. In the summer, they are very dry. The highest mountain in northern Africa, Mount Toubkal, rises 13,665 feet (4,165 meters) high.

Mount Toubkal is covered with snow in the winter, but most of it melts in summer.

Sand dunes in the Sahara can reach more than 490 feet (150 m) high.

To the south and east of the mountains lies the Sahara. The Sahara is the world's largest desert. It covers more than 3,630,000 square miles (9,400,000 square kilometers). That is almost as big as the United States! During the day, the weather is very hot. The temperature gets up to 115°F (45°C). Then, at night, it cools down to around 75°F (24°C).

Natural Resources

Morocco has many phosphate mines. Phosphate is a rock. People use it in fertilizer to help plants grow. Other countries buy phosphate from Morocco.

A worker uses a crane to move phosphate at a mine in Western Sahara.

Farmers grow fruits and vegetables for the people of Morocco and other countries. Oranges, lemons, and tangerines are popular. Tangerines are named after the Moroccan city of Tangier.

A worker harvests oranges from a grove in southern Morocco.

Special Trees

Argan trees grow only in a few places in the world. They grow near the base of some mountain ranges in Morocco. Moroccans harvest the trees' nuts to make oil.

Argan and almond trees dot the foothills of the Anti-Atlas Mountains.

Goats like to eat the leaves on argan trees. But the leaves grow too high for the goats to reach. So the goats climb up the trunk. Then they stand on the tree branches to eat their tasty snack. Tree goats are quite a sight to see!

Tree goats snack on an argan tree.

The Berber People

Most of the people who live in Morocco are from one of two ethnic groups. The people of an ethnic group share a religion, a history, and a language. The Berber people have lived in Morocco for more than four thousand years. They were farmers and herders.

Berber shepherds watch their flocks in central Morocco.

Berber groups mostly lived in or near the mountains. They left many cave paintings. The paintings tell us what their life was like. Many modern-day Berbers still live in the Moroccan mountains.

Berbers created this rock painting more than three thousand years ago.

The Arab People

The Arab people are the largest ethnic group in Morocco. They came to Morocco long ago. The Arabs wanted to teach people about their religion, Islam.

This young Arab woman lives in the central Moroccan city of Marrakech.

Arabs lived in Morocco's larger cities. Soon many Berbers adopted Islam as their religion. Some Berbers started speaking Arabic, the Arab language. Most modern-day Moroccans are part Arab.

These schoolchildren in Casablanca are preparing to visit the national mosque, or Islamic house of worship.

21

Religion

Islam is the official religion of Morocco. Nearly all Moroccans are Muslims and follow the Islamic faith.

24

Islam is an important part of Moroccan life. Muslims celebrate many religious holidays. These include Eid al-Fitr and Eid al-Adha.

Ramadan

Ramadan is an important time for Muslims. It lasts for one month. During Ramadan, grown-up Muslims do not eat or drink between sunrise and sunset. When the sun goes down, they eat. They eat another meal before sunrise. Families celebrate the end of the month with a three-day feast called Eid al-Fitr.

People crowd a pastry stand in Rabat during Ramadan. They will eat the pastries after the sun goes down.

Language

Morocco's official language is Arabic. The Moroccan style of Arabic is called *darija*. It differs from Arabic spoken in other countries. A Moroccan and a person from Syria may both speak Arabic. But they would have a hard time understanding each other.

Most Moroccans speak Arabic. These women are in Marrakech.

In some small villages, people might speak a native Berber language. A few different Berber languages exist in Morocco. Some Moroccans also speak French, Spanish, and English.

How to Say It in Arabic

hello	AH-hlan
good-bye	MAH ahs-sah-LEH-mah
please	min FUD-luk
thank you	SHUK-rahn
Morocco	el-MAH-greb

This man is carving Arabic into a piece of marble.

The King

A king leads Morocco's government. Mohammed VI became king in 1999. He is also the religious leader of Morocco. King Mohammed VI wants Morocco to be a modern country with good relations with other countries.

King Mohammed VI takes part in a ceremony in honor of a visiting president in 2006.

He wants good education and health care for Moroccans. He also wants to improve the way women are treated. King Mohammed VI thinks that women should be educated and have jobs outside the home if they want.

The royal palace is also called the Dar el-Makhzen.

The Royal City

The king lives in this grand palace in the royal city of Rabat. Rabat is the capital of Morocco.

Casablanca was founded more than two thousand years ago.

Living in the City

Moroccan cities are big, busy, and filled with people. Casablanca is the largest city. The word *casablanca* means "white house" in Spanish. And many white buildings fill the city. But Casablanca also has many slums. Slums are crowded, dirty areas of a city. Many poor people live there.

Moroccans who live in cities work in many different jobs. They might work in offices, restaurants, shops, or factories. Factory workers make clothes, furniture, plastics, and machines.

These women work at a clothing factory in Tangier.

Living in the Country

Less than half the people in Morocco live in the country. Some live on small farms. They grow rice, cotton, fruits, and other crops. They also raise sheep and goats. Other people live in villages built on the sides of mountains. Near the desert, people live in tent villages.

This Berber village is on a hillside in the Atlas Mountains.

This Berber tribe lives in a tent village in the Sahara.

In the country, people grow or make what they need. They produce their own food and catch fish to eat. They make their clothes. If they don't have something they need, they trade with others.

Family Is Everything

Family life is important to Moroccans. Families are very close and help one another.

This Moroccan family is eating a traditional meal.

If you lived in Morocco, you would probably live with your parents, brothers and sisters, grandparents, and maybe even your uncles, aunts, and cousins. Does that sound like a crowded house? Well, you would always have someone to play with.

Pastimes

Families in Morocco like to spend time together. They might go hunting, play golf, or just go for a walk. They also like to play soccer, the most popular sport in Morocco. Soccer is also the national sport.

Young people play soccer near a city wall in southern Morocco.

School

Children in Morocco go to primary school from the age of seven to the age of thirteen. They learn reading, writing, math, and science. But in small villages, many children cannot go to school. They may not have a school that is close to them. Sometimes there are not enough teachers.

This classroom is in the city of Fez in northern Morocco.

34

Some children stop going to school when they are thirteen. They might need to help on the family farm. Or they need to work to help support their family. Sometimes, girls stay home to help with younger children or to take care of the home.

Rights for Women

In Morocco, men have more rights than women. Many Moroccans think that a boy's education is more important than a girl's. Often girls do not stay in school. Many women do not work outside the home. But this is starting to change. More Moroccan girls are getting an education. They are becoming doctors and working in business and government.

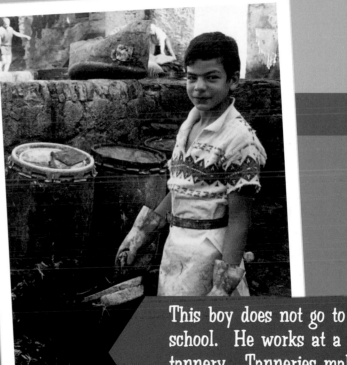

This boy does not go to school. He works at a tannery. Tanneries make leather from animal skin.

Food

Moroccan food has many delicious flavors! Cooks use lots of spices, fruit, and nuts. Lamb, chicken, goat, and fish are favorite main dishes. They are served with couscous (steamed wheat), the national dish. Moroccans also eat bread at every meal. They use flat bread to scoop up meat and vegetables.

A restaurant in Marrakech serves this dish of couscous and vegetables.

Moroccans love to eat pastries made with almonds, dates, and figs. They also like other sweet desserts. The desserts are often flavored with orange blossoms or rose petals and then soaked in honey.

The National Drink

Moroccans drink hot mint tea in small glasses. They add sugar to sweeten the tea. Making tea for friends and family is an important part of daily life.

These men are enjoying traditional mint tea.

Carpets and Crafts

Hundreds of beautiful crafts are for sale in Morocco's outdoor markets. Artists sell colorful, handmade pottery with detailed designs. Leather workers offer sandals and bags made from goatskins and sheepskins. Moroccan women sell and wear lots of silver bracelets, necklaces, and pins.

This market in Marrakech bustles with activity.

This rug shop is
in a southwestern
Moroccan city.

Rugs and carpets are the most important Moroccan crafts.
For hundreds of years, families have passed down the skills
and the patterns for weaving the carpets' designs.

Music

Moroccans enjoy many different kinds of music. Berber music comes from long ago and often tells stories. Berber musicians play flutes and drums. Many people love to dance to their music.

Berber musicians perform in a city square.

Chaabi music is a mix of different styles. At the end of a chaabi song, the musicians play it again, twice as fast. People clap, shout, and dance!

Rai is a modern type of music. It sounds like rock music heard on the radio in the United States. Musicians use electric guitars, drums, and other rock instruments.

Holidays

Moroccans hold many regional festivals to celebrate yearly farm activities. For example, the almond blossom season and the harvesting of fruits such as oranges, dates, olives, and tomatoes are all reasons to celebrate.

These women are performing at the Rose Festival in the Grand Atlas Mountains.

42

Throne Day on July 30 is a national holiday in Morocco. It honors the day Mohammed VI became the king. On this day, leaders from all over the world congratulate the king. King Mohammed VI makes a speech to the people of Morocco. They celebrate with parades, dances, food, and fireworks.

Moroccans cheer the king during a Throne Day celebration.

43

THE FLAG OF MOROCCO

Morocco's flag is red with a green, five-pointed star in the center. Red and green are colors that are often used in Arab flags. The star is called the Seal of Solomon. It stands for the country's devotion to Islam and for life, wisdom, and good health.

FAST FACTS

FULL COUNTRY NAME: Kingdom of Morocco

AREA: 172,413 square miles (446,550 square kilometers). That is a little bigger than the state of California.

MAIN LANDFORMS: the mountain ranges Anti-Atlas, Er Rif, Grand Atlas, and Middle Atlas; the desert Sahara; high plateaus; valleys; lowlands

MAJOR RIVERS: Bou Regreg, Moulouya, Oum er Rbia, Rheris, Sebou, Sous, Tensift, and Ziz

ANIMALS AND THEIR HABITATS: hedgehogs, jackals, porcupines, rabbits, (coasts and plains); mountain cats, sheep, wild boars (highlands); eagles, hawks, monkeys, owls, vultures (mountains); desert fox, hyenas, jackals, rats, scorpions, snakes, squirrels (desert); dolphins, fish, monk seals, porpoises (seacoast).

CAPITAL CITY: Rabat

OFFICIAL LANGUAGE: Arabic

POPULATION: about 31,285,200

GLOSSARY

capital: a city where the government of a state or country is located

continent: any one of seven large areas of land. The continents are Africa, Antarctica, Asia, Australia, Europe, North America, and South America.

desert: a dry, sandy region

ethnic group: a group of people with many things in common, such as language, religion, history, and customs

mountain: a part of Earth's surface that rises high into the sky

natural resources: things that are supplied by nature and are useful to people

plain: a big area of flat land

territory: land that is under the control of a government

TO LEARN MORE

BOOKS

Alalou, Elizabeth, and Ali Alalou. *The Butter Man*. Watertown, MA: Charlesbridge Publishing, 2008. This picture book captures the Moroccan culture and landscape through a story about patience, perseverance, and hope.

Douglas, Susan. *Ramadan*. Minneapolis: Millbrook Press, 2004. Look at the history of and customs surrounding Ramadan.

Raabe, Emily. *A Primary Source Guide to Morocco*. New York: PowerKids Press, 2005. This book gives a brief overview of Morocco's past and present.

Riley, Nancy. *Moroccan Mystery*. Bloomington, IN: iUniverse, 2008. Learn about Islam, Moroccan culture, and the trade in endangered animal products in this book.

WEBSITES

Time for Kids around the World: Morocco
http://www.timeforkids.com/TFK/teachers/aw/wr/article/0,28138,1983086,00.html
Explore Morocco and celebrate the culture, people, landmarks, and geography.

Yahoo! KIDS
http://kids.yahoo.com/reference/world-factbook/country/mo
World Factbook contains maps, pictures of flags, statistics, and information on Morocco's history, land, people, government, and money.

INDEX